20 CIRCULAR WALKS IN ESSEX

Len Banister

COUNTRYSIDE BOOKS
NEWBURY BERKSHIRE

First published 2023
© 2023 Len Banister

All rights reserved. No part of this publication may be reproduced, stored in a retrieval system, or transmitted by any means, electronic, mechanical, photocopying, recording or otherwise, without the prior written permission of the copyright holder and publishers.

COUNTRYSIDE BOOKS
3 Catherine Road
Newbury, Berkshire, RG14 7NA

To view our complete range of books please visit us at
www.countrysidebooks.co.uk

ISBN 978 1 84674 423 5

All materials used in the manufacture of this book carry FSC certification.

Produced by The Letterworks Ltd., Reading
Designed and Typeset by KT Designs, St Helens
Printed by Holywell Press, Oxford

Introduction

Over the last few years, we have become increasingly aware of how important walking, especially in the countryside, is to our physical and mental wellbeing. Essex, with its extensive network of public rights of way, offers excellent opportunities to visit villages, castles, rivers, woodlands, and seashores, plus a whole host of other attractions.

This selection of walks is intended not only to sample many of the riches that Essex has, but also to encourage families to walk together as a social occasion. As a result, most of the walks are flat and many include playgrounds or other opportunities for adventure.

The directions are written so that, especially with the small map included, you should have no difficulty in following the route. Each outing includes a place to park and a pub or café for refreshment. Stopping along the way to buy food or drink does wonders for the local economy and ensures that the diminishing number of food outlets, particularly pubs, survive.

20 Circular Walks in Essex

The footpaths and tracks that we use are all part of the living countryside and subject to growth and the weather – if you encounter difficulties en route, please take the time to contact the Essex Highway Authority at www.essexhighways.org/tell-us and the Area Footpath Secretary of the Ramblers charity at www.essexarearamblers.co.uk.

I hope you enjoy these walks and thank all those who help to keep our pathways accessible. I also thank Julie, my wife, for all the assistance she has given in designing and evaluating these excursions.

Len Banister

Publisher's Note

We hope that you obtain considerable enjoyment from this book; great care has been taken in its preparation. Although at the time of publication all routes followed public rights of way or permitted paths, diversion orders can be made and permissions withdrawn.

We cannot, of course, be held responsible for such diversion orders or any inaccuracies in the text which result from these or any other changes to the routes, nor any damage which might result from walkers trespassing on private property. We are anxious, though, that all the details covering the walks are kept up to date, and would therefore welcome information from readers which would be relevant to future editions.

The simple sketch maps that accompany the walks in this book are based on notes made by the author whilst surveying the routes on the ground. They are designed to show you how to reach the start and to point out the main features of the overall circuit, and they contain a progression of numbers that relate to the paragraphs of the text.

However, for the benefit of a proper map, we do recommend that you purchase the relevant Ordnance Survey sheet covering your walk. Ordnance Survey maps are widely available, especially through booksellers and local newsagents.

1 Saffron Walden & Audley End

4 miles (6.3 km)

Start: Swan Meadow Car Park, Park Lane, Saffron Walden. **Sat Nav:** CB10 1DA.
Parking: The Swan Meadow pay and display car park is brown-signed off the B184 north-west of the town.
Map: OS Explorer 195 Braintree & Saffron Walden. **Grid Ref:** TL534385.
Terrain: Streets, pavements, and grassy paths. One longish stretch along the road to ensure the view of Audley End House. Can be managed with pushchairs and dogs.

WALK HIGHLIGHTS

The walk starts with a brief tour of Saffron Walden, taking in the castle, the museum and two of the four mazes for which, beside the historic trade in saffron, the town is famous. We quickly go forth into the parkland of Audley End House. The original building dates from the 17th century, but in the 1780s Robert Adam remodelled the house whilst Capability Brown got to work on the gardens – the result is one of the iconic sights of Essex. This walk is rich in outing possibilities, and it is likely that you will want to return for the house, the town and the railway, quite apart from the numerous parkland walks you could devise.

20 Circular Walks in Essex

REFRESHMENTS
The Eight Bells, which you pass on Bridge Street early in the walk, oozes olde-worlde charm and has a menu packed with pub classics.
🌐 www.theeightbellssaffronwalden.com ☎ 01799 522790

THE WALK
❶ Go to the far, eastern end of the car park. Turn right, passing the Swan Meadow Maze and take the first turning left past a pond and follow the high wall on the right. Continue to the High Street which you cross and turn left, passing the Eight Bells pub on your right. Soon turn right into Bridge End Gardens. Go left at a T-junction, then right through the gate guarded by eagles and walk forward amid the topiary. Emerge at a T-junction and take a wide path to the right. Keep forward past decorative gates to reach Castle Street.

❷ Turn left, and then right along Museum Street. Take the first turning left, passing medieval stone coffins and the Saffron Walden Museum to go diagonally right across the grass, passing the 12th-century Walden Castle and continue down to a gate and road. Cross the roads to go diagonally right across the common; aim for a point about 40m to the left of the children's playground. Arrive at Saffron's famous 17th-century Turf Maize, which is about 40m in length, with a path to the centre of 1500m. Turn around and walk back, aiming for the left of the car park in front of you. Reach a road where you turn left and then right along Hill Street (there are toilets here). Cross the High Street and head along Abbey Lane, passing magnificent almshouses to reach the entrance to Audley End Estate.

❸ Once through the gate, take the left fork and keep forward ignoring

Walk 1 – **Saffron Walden & Audley End**

all side paths to reach another gate and a road (Audley End Road). Turn right and follow this road, with borders designated as a roadside nature reserve, for about ¾ mile. At the bottom of the road, on the right, you pass the entrance to Audley End House (English Heritage) and, on the left, the entrance to Audley End Miniature Railway. Keep forward over the ornamental bridge to a road junction.

4 Turn right. Look over the ha-ha to see the grand house across the lake. *On your left, up the hill, there is Ring Temple, which was erected to commemorate the Treaty of Paris at the end of the Seven Years' War in 1763. Further along on the right are the superb Audley End Stables, rivalling in beauty the house itself.* Pass the gatehouse with the bull heads and continue along the pavement to the end of the flint wall.

5 Turn right at a fingerpost, signed to Home Farm. Cross the river and then go right, down a slope, at a waymarker to walk alongside a stream. Emerge onto parkland and fork slightly right, away from the stream and towards a gap in the hedge ahead. Over your right shoulder you can see the back of the house. Keep ahead in the next field, swinging gradually right. At the next junction of paths, go left and, at a T-junction, go right. Cross a bridge and fork left. Turn left at the next fork to return to your car.

2 Bartlow Hills
4 miles (6.3 km)

Start: Camps Lane, Bartlow. **Sat Nav:** CB21 4PP.
Parking: Roadside parking on Camps Lane to the east of the village, near the church. Park alongside, not in, the high-walled courtyard.
Map: OS Explorer 209 Cambridge; Royston, Duxford & Linton. **Grid Ref:** TL586452.
Terrain: There are several gentle climbs, mainly along good tracks. Field-edge sections can be muddy in winter. All-terrain pushchairs will manage the route. Dog-friendly. Look out for deer tracks.

WALK HIGHLIGHTS

Starting in the pretty village of Bartlow, and with a brief foray into Cambridgeshire, this walk quickly returns to Essex and takes you gradually up the side of the River Bourn valley to provide glorious views, enhanced by masses of wild flowers in the spring and early summer. The return is equally attractive, but the most astonishing feature is saved until the last. Emerging from woodland you are suddenly confronted by huge Roman burial mounds. Burial mounds for the ashes of top officials were a common feature of Roman settlements but these are the largest of any found in Europe. Dating from the 1st century they were seriously damaged by Victorian archaeologists hunting for, and finding, treasure. Now in the care of local trustees and Cambridge County Council, their future is more secure.

Walk 2 – **Bartlow Hills**

REFRESHMENTS
The Three Hills, an award-winning gastro pub with marvellous food and a super children's menu, is just around the corner from the start of the walk.
🌐 www.thethreehills.co.uk ☎ 01223 890500

THE WALK
❶ With the church behind you, turn left along Camps Road towards the crossroads where you turn left along Ashdon Road heading for the Three Hills pub. Keep ahead past the pub to reach another crossroads and turn right along Bartlow Road. *On this quiet, attractive lane the embankment of a dismantled railway looms high up on the left. The railway, which was part of the Stour Valley Line, was opened in 1865 and closed in 1967 as part of the Beeching cuts.* Swing left between the remains of a bridge and continue along the lane to take a byway on the left uphill. In ¼ mile, near the top, you meet a curved, wide track.

❷ Turn left, guided by a red waymarker. Soon, at a fork, go right. Your climb will be rewarded by spectacular views over the surrounding countryside. Ignore the junction which is opposite the settlement of Aulnoye and continue on what has now become a semi-surfaced lane going slightly uphill to cross a bridge over the almost expunged railbed. Ignore the next footpath on the right and follow the lane around to the left to reach a road (Bartlow Road).

❸ Turn left and immediately right at a fingerpost. Pass a sports field to join a farm track. At a fork, go left to continue with the wood to your right. In ¼ mile, arrive at a complex junction and take the second path on the left – a section of the Harcamlow Way. Ignore a raised crossfield path on the left and climb to the next boundary.

❹ Turn left on a farm track. After losing most of the height you have gained during the walk you approach a road. About 15m before it, turn right. Pass the elegant water tower and swing left. Just before the road, take steps up to your right to follow a short woodland path (anyone unable to climb the steps should continue to the road, turn right and go right at a waymarker) cross a lane and go right on a narrow, hedged path. Go through a gate and to your right you will see what appear to be two giant anthills. *These are two of the remaining six Roman burial mounds in the vicinity.* Follow the path to the right of the information board then walk between

20 Circular Walks in Essex

the mounds; the one on the right has steps enabling you to climb to the top without damaging it. Turn left in front of the fence, alongside the cutting of another branch of the disused railway. Cross a bridge and turn left into the churchyard to follow the path to the main road and your car.

3 Stansted Mountfitchet
5 miles (8 km)

Start: Lower Street Car Park, Church Road, Stansted Mountfitchet. **Sat Nav:** CM24 8PU.
Parking: Lower Street pay and display car park is situated near the station. It is zoned for particular users, and you are advised to park towards the far end, past the skate-board park.
Map: OS Explorer 195 Braintree & Saffron Walden. **Grid Ref:** TL517249.
Terrain: Some gradual climbs and descents along field edges and quiet lanes. A short 280m section along the pavement by a busy road at section 2. Overall, all-terrain pushchair-friendly but there is a 30m section where the chair would have to be carried because of mud. Dog-friendly.

WALK HIGHLIGHTS
When you arrive at the car park you will immediately see Mountfitchet Castle. This amazing reconstruction of a Norman castle provides hands-on experiences for the young and not-so-young, and is well worth a visit.

20 Circular Walks in Essex

The walk itself leaves the busy town and is soon in beautiful countryside, passing grand Essex houses along the way. On the return leg you'll get the chance to see an early 18th-century windmill.

REFRESHMENTS
The Three Horseshoes, roughly half-way round the route, makes for the perfect refreshment stop.
🌐 www.threehorseshoeshazelend.co.uk ☎ 01279 813429

THE WALK

❶ Head out of the car park and take the first left uphill at the roundabout. Near the top of the hill, turn right along Park Road. At the end, go left along ornamental railings and emerge on a lane (you will glimpse the windmill that we visit later). Keep forward down a narrow path when the lane goes left. Emerge on a road (West Road), continuing left. At a junction, go right uphill over the railway to the main road with the Old Bell on the right.

❷ Turn left along the pavement for 280m of this busy road. Cross right to go down Limekiln Lane. Take a right fork with scenic views to the left. Reach a junction and take a tight left down Watermill Lane and over the River Stort. Pass the remains of defunct watercress beds at the bottom of the valley on the right. When the lane turns sharply left, climb the bank to walk up the right edge of the field along a line of oak trees. At the top, turn for the view then continue through a gap to cross a cricket field and reach a road (Hazel End Road). This is the hamlet of Hazel End with its attractive houses, duck pond and a vineyard. The Three Horseshoes is on your left.

❸ To continue the walk, however, you turn right, signed for Manuden. Just after passing the lodge for Hassobury, look for a fingerpost on the right. Don't go down into the sunken path but walk along the right field-edge. At the bottom, cross a track and go forward on a narrow path. This section is likely to be muddy. Emerge from the wood and turn left, and then go right on a grassy track passing an attractive cluster of trees. At a junction of tracks, swing left toward barns. Just before Hole Farm, turn left along a permissive track between the barns to join a footpath and go right to a junction of lanes.

❹ Take the second turning left and follow the lane until it swings right. Go left at a fingerpost. Keep to the right of the hedge ahead to follow the left

Walk 3 – **Stansted Mountfitchet**

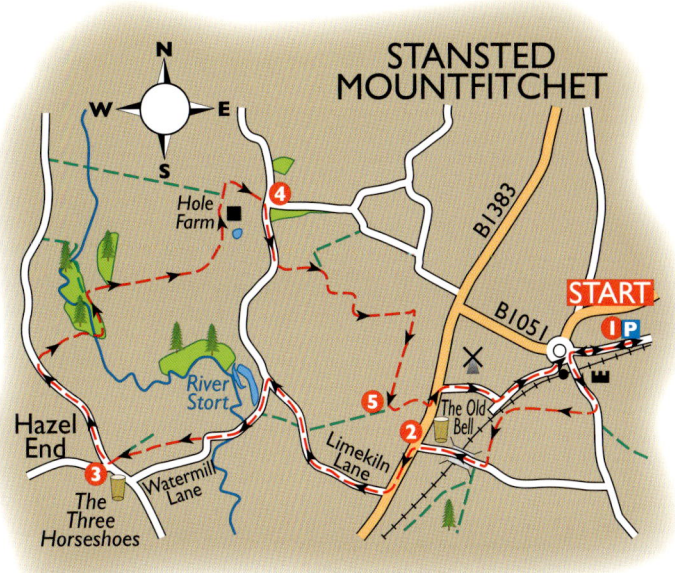

field-edge as it zig-zags for nearly ½ mile. Then, go right along the backs of houses and eventually arrive at a crosstrack.

5 Turn left along a fenced path to reach a road (Silver Street). Cross and go left and then turn right, signed 'windmill' which suddenly appears on your left. Continue down Mill Hill, following it to a T-junction (Brook Road) where you go left. Turn right along the signed footpath just to the left of house number 5. Cross the bridge and go left along Water Lane. At the station, go left to take the second turning right at the roundabout and return to your car.

4 Thaxted & Cutlers Green

4 miles (6.3 km)

Start: Margaret Street Car Park, Thaxted. **Sat Nav:** CM6 2RL.
Parking: Margaret Street Car Park is signed off the B184 and is a large free car park with toilets available.
Map: OS Explorer 195 Braintree & Saffron Walden. **Grid Ref:** TL611312.
Terrain: Some surfaced paths but mainly field edges, suitable for all-terrain pushchairs. Dog-friendly.

WALK HIGHLIGHTS

Thaxted is a well-preserved little town and arguably one of the most attractive in Essex. It sits on relatively high ground so that two of its jewels, the church and the windmill, can be seen for miles around. Another major attraction, the magnificent 15th-century Guildhall, features toward the end of this walk – the building perfectly represents the town's historic prosperity, which was built on industries associated with cutlery and wool. The early stage of the walk follows the juvenile River Chelmer and then branches out into open countryside punctuated by delightful secluded, covered paths.

Walk 4 – **Thaxted & Cutlers Green**

REFRESHMENTS
The Swan, which you'll reach early in the walk, is a traditional coaching inn with open fires, oak beams and an appealing menu.
🌐 www.greeneking-pubs.co.uk/pubs/essex/swan-hotel/ ☎ 01371 830321

THE WALK

❶ Leaving the car park turn right uphill to the main road where you turn left. At the junction, with the Swan on the left, go right down Watling Lane. Follow the lane for about ½ mile. The surface gradually deteriorates. *The lane is on the Harcamlow Way which is a 141-mile trail developed by members of the Ramblers and re-signed by the Redbridge Group.* Eventually cross a bridge with metal railings on the left.

❷ Turn left along the field-edge with the juvenile River Chelmer on the left. Cross a farm track with a concrete bridge on the left and continue, with the river, on the left edge of a large field. Arrive at a junction with bridges left and ahead.

❸ Turn right on a left field-edge to climb a crossfield path in the next field. At the top a bench has been thoughtfully placed to enable you to rest and admire the view back to Thaxted. Go right and then left to follow a glorious track down to the hamlet of Cutlers Green. *The 'Cutlers' is a reference to the cutlery industry in the Middle Ages.* Keep forward past a house to a road.

❹ Turn left. Cross the main road (Cutlers Green Lane), continuing with the green on the right. Just past the pond, go left at a fingerpost along a path. This is often muddy at first but develops into a delightful tree-lined trail which joins a left field-edge. Swing left between a group of trees and continue to reach a metal gate. Pass to the left and walk along the field-edge which becomes fenced. Pass through a metal gate and go for a short distance on a drive before climbing left up a shallow bank by a waymarker. Keep ahead to reach the main road.

❺ Turn left over a bridge and immediately left and then right on a field-edge. Ahead is a glorious view of the church and windmill in Thaxted. Keep

20 Circular Walks in Essex

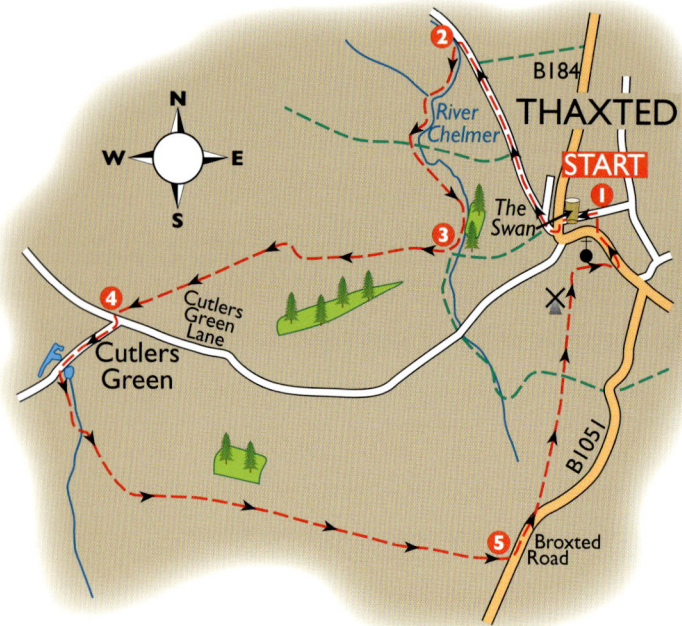

forward for ½ mile to pass to the right of the windmill. Follow the surfaced path through a kissing gate between the cemetery and houses to fork right and continue down Fishmarket Street, turning left at the Guildhall. Continue up Town Street. Opposite the Church of St John the Baptist with Our Lady and St Laurence turn right along Bell Lane. Turn right and then left to return to the car park.

5 Castle Hedingham
4 miles (6.3 km)

Start: The Bell, St James's Street, Castle Hedingham. **Sat Nav:** CO9 3EJ.
Parking: Park roadside on St James's Street near the Bell.
Map: OS Explorer 195 Braintree & Saffron Walden. **Grid Ref:** TL786356.
Terrain: Some gradual climbing, mostly on good tracks but field edges can be very muddy in winter or after heavy rain. All-terrain pushchairs should manage the route. Dog-friendly.

WALK HIGHLIGHTS

While there are many attractive villages in Essex, this walk starts and finishes in one of the most wonderful. The contrasting styles of architecture, including many medieval timber-framed buildings painted in beautiful pastel hues, makes it particularly special. Beyond the village, you'll stride out along the water meadows of the River Colne, passing the Railway Museum, before a gradual climb out of the valley rewards you with views of countryside stretching for miles. The return provides enticing glimpses of 11th-century Hedingham Castle. The keep, which is all that remains, was built in the 12th century and is thought to be the best preserved Norman keep in England.

20 Circular Walks in Essex

REFRESHMENTS
The Bell is worth a visit just to tour the 15th and 16th-century honeycomb of rooms. It has a massive menu that changes daily (closed Tuesdays).
🌐 www.hedinghambell.co.uk ☎ 01787 460350

THE WALK
❶ With your back to the Bell, go left past the tea rooms and turn right along King Street. At the junction, head along Church Ponds. Turn right at Crown Street to reach the main road where you turn left. At a fork, turn right on Kirby Hall Road. After passing a school, the road narrows without a pavement. *The Colne Valley on the left supports sheep whilst the rising fields on the right are nearly all arable.* After about ½ mile on this road you reach a metal sheepfold.

❷ Go left to a fingerpost, then right along a left field-edge. At the boundary, cross a bridge and go left on the field-edge, ignoring a stile, to continue with extensive views of the Colne Valley Railway. *This can be visited from the A1017. Besides the rolling-stock you can see, there is a miniature railway, a museum and the chance to take a trip on the short length of railway.* The path swings gradually right. At a corner where a path emerges from Poole Farm you go right to begin a gradual climb. At a junction turn right and then left to continue on a broad farm track with a hedge and ditch on your right. The track swings right at the top to approach farm buildings. Continue on hard standing.

❸ Turn right in front of the first barn, and then go left after the office. Pass

Walk 5 – Castle Hedingham

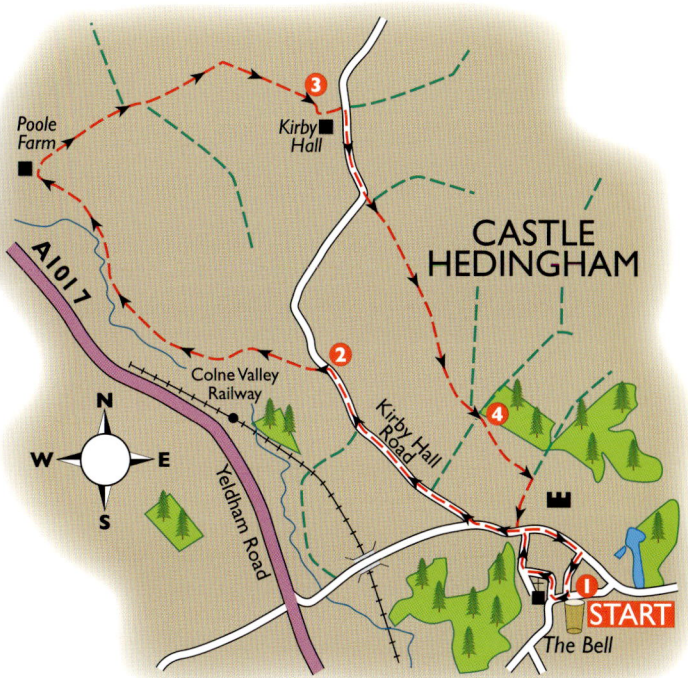

16th-century Kirby Hall and reach a lane. Turn right. Where the lane goes sharply right by the Warren, go straight on with a fingerpost. At the end of the first field, join the left edge of the next, passing under power lines to reach a complex junction.

❹ After the hedge, take the path which is going right downhill. Over to the left, you get a good view of the castle. Arrive at a T-junction, and go right to the main road where you turn left. Keep forward to crossroads; on the left is the entrance to the castle. Turn right along Castle Lane and keep forward at the junction to reach St James's Street to return to your car and the pub.

6 Dedham

2¾ miles (4.3 km)

Start: Mill Lane Dedham Car Park, Dedham. **Sat Nav:** CO7 6DJ.
Parking: The pay and display car park on Mill Lane is just north of Dedham Church.
Map: OS Explorer 196 Sudbury, Hadleigh & Dedham Vale. **Grid Ref:** TM058334.
Terrain: This is an easy, flat walk although there are some uneven surfaces. In autumn and winter there is the possibility that the River Stour will flood, and it is likely that some areas of riverside will become very wet so boots might be useful. Dog-friendly.

WALK HIGHLIGHTS

Dedham is a delightful centre for walks; the village itself with its well-preserved Georgian and Tudor architecture is a visitors' delight. Set in the valley of the River Stour it offers a wide range of opportunities to visit the scenes chosen by John Constable, one of Britain's greatest landscape painters. This route offers something for all seasons; in the spring the

Walk 6 – **Dedham**

riverbanks are strewn with flowers and the willows are displaying their new shoots; in summer the cattle are out on the floodplain consuming the rich grass; autumn and winter bring new energy to the river providing strong currents and rushing streams.

REFRESHMENTS
The Sun Inn is an upmarket pub and restaurant serving excellent, locally sourced food. ⊕ www.thesuninndedham.com ☎ 01206 323351. Alternatively, try the Marlborough, also passed on the walk and equally good. ⊕ www.themarlboroughgroup.co.uk ☎ 01672 515011

THE WALK
❶ Return to Mill Lane and turn right. Immediately after passing the converted mill, turn left at a fingerpost along a brick-surfaced path to pass the mill pond and cross the millrace. Go down steps, through a gate and turn left along the meadow. The River Stour is now over to your left and you are walking along its floodplain with a fence to the right. Pass a boathouse disguised as a temple on the far bank of the river. After a metal kissing gate you are closer to the river and the plain is open to the right – in the distance you can glimpse the Church of Stratford St Mary nestling in the trees. *Trees along this part of the walk are the stars; the willows lining the banks of the river are all pollarded. When freshly cut they are stumpy, at the time of writing they haven't been trimmed for 10 years. If their wood is not harvested between 15 to 20 years, they become top*

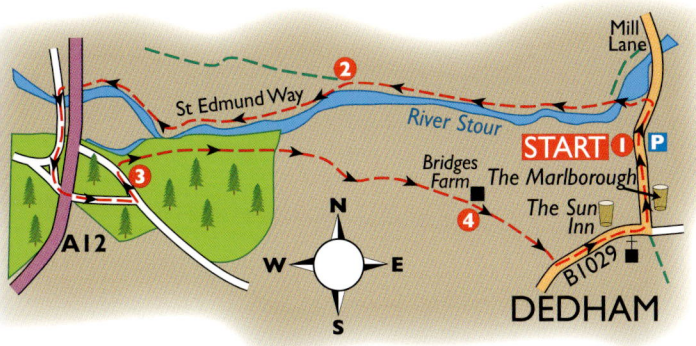

20 Circular Walks in Essex

heavy and buckle over. In wintertime, massive bunches of mistletoe are revealed on the branches of taller trees. When you reach a waymarker, fork left.

❷ Keep close to the riverbank and cross a bridge over a stream. In just over ¼ mile you reach a metal gate and go through a tunnel under the A12. At the road turn left to cross the bridge over the River Stour with the manicured grounds of Talbooth Restaurant below. Keep left at the junction and continue over the A12. Turn left along a drive to Milsoms, now on the Essex Way.

❸ Opposite the house, go right, initially steeply, along a narrow path and keep forward through a gap in the fence to walk with the River Stour to your left as you enter a National Trust area via a kissing gate. The path moves further away from the river and you enter the left-hand edge of a larger field where the predominant trees are oaks. Dedham church now dominates the view ahead. Reach the buildings of Bridges Farm.

❹ Swing slightly right to join a hedged track and reach the main road (High Street). Go left. *This short walk to the centre of the village is a real treat; the variety of styles and colours of the houses, sprinkled with small shops and tea rooms is reminiscent of the way small towns used to look prior to new developments.* Pass the church with the Sun Inn opposite and turn left down Mill Lane by the Marlborough pub to find the car park entrance on the right-hand side.

7 Colchester

2½ miles (4 km)

Start: Greyfriars Hotel Car Park, Castle Road, Colchester. **Sat Nav:** CO1 1UR.
Parking: The pay and display car park on Castle Road, opposite the Foresters Arms.
Map: OS Explorer 184 Colchester. **Grid Ref:** TM001254.
Terrain: Streets and surfaced paths, some inclines. Dog-friendly.

WALK HIGHLIGHTS

Presently home to battalions of the Parachute Regiment, Colchester has, since Roman times, been a military town. The Romans made Colchester their capital and this walk follows much of the 2.5m thick wall that the invaders built. The history of the town is interestingly explained by the many information boards located along the route. You'll finish by visiting Castle Park, which not only houses Roman remains but also features a magnificent 11th-century castle, now a museum. A massive play area will be of interest to younger walkers.

20 Circular Walks in Essex

REFRESHMENTS
The Foresters Arms, at the start of the walk, is a charming, welcoming pub for all the family.
🌐 www.theforestersarmscolchester.co.uk ☎ 01206 899791

THE WALK

❶ Leave the car park, facing the Foresters Arms, turn right and continue right along Roman Road to a T-junction. Go left and use a crossing to turn right along Priory Street. *Here you will get your first glimpse of the Roman Wall, parts of which show repairs carried out in the 12th century.* Just before a T-junction, divert left to wander through the ruins of the 12th-century St Botolph's Priory. Continue to the junction.

❷ Turn right and take the first left along Short Wyre Street. As this swings right, carry straight on along the bustling Eid Lane (there are toilets on the right). Continue along Sir Isaac's Walk to a junction.

❸ Cross, turn left and then swing right along Crouch Street. At the T-junction, turn right and walk uphill, using the footpath, along the best-surviving section of the wall, passing steps to a church which is now an arts centre. Reach the Balkerne Gate which was the largest Roman gateway in Britain, beyond which is a magnificent water tower and the Mercury Theatre. At the top of the hill swing right to the site of what was the North Gate.

❹ Cross the road to St Peter's Street and keep forward to a junction. Go

Walk 7 – **Colchester**

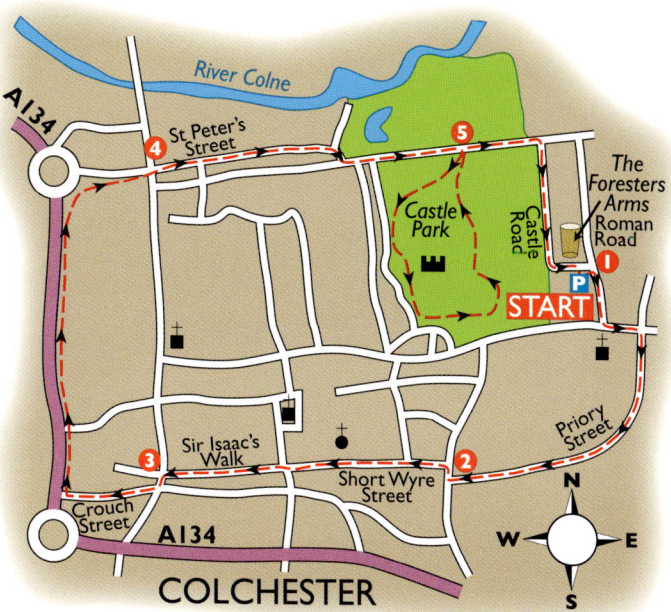

right for a few metres along Middle Mill, and then turn left through Rye Gate. At a path junction, turn right with a boating lake to your left (there are toilets here) and continue to join a hedged path.

5 At the first junction, go right. Now keep to the main path, the turnings on the left enable you to visit the bandstand, the site of Roman town houses and a café. Keep forward between gardens to reach the 11th-century Colchester Castle. Follow the path left in front of the castle and keep forward to pass Hollytrees Museum. Keep to this path passing steps and taking the higher of two routes. Pass between two large play areas (there are toilets here). At the next junction go left and then right to re-join the wall where you turn right. Reach a narrow arch and turn right through it to walk up Castle Road. At the top turn left then go right to return to the car park.

8 The Naze
4 or 5 miles (6.4 or 7.9 km)

> **Start:** Naze Car Park, Sunny Point, Walton-on-the-Naze. **Sat Nav:** CO14 8LF.
> **Parking:** The pay and display car park near the Naze Tower.
> **Map:** OS Explorer 184 Colchester. **Grid Ref:** TM265234.
> **Terrain:** The path along the sea wall deteriorates and becomes narrow and uneven, you can walk below the path along an easy grassy track but then you lose the advantage of height and views. It is a good idea to wrap up warmly against winds. Dog-friendly.

WALK HIGHLIGHTS
This walk includes the wild countryside and vast stretches of water on the sea wall's periphery that make the Naze unique. The area is a dream for birdwatchers. Then there's the Naze Tower, constructed in 1720 as a lighthouse and now open to the public as a tea room and museum in the summer. Look out for the array of information boards and don't forget the binoculars. Oh, and make sure you come back with a snap or two of the colourful beach huts.

REFRESHMENTS
The Bath House is among a number of options in Walton-on-the-Naze – the Sunday roasts are a particular highlight.
🌐 facebook.com/bathhousepub   ☎ 01255 675848

Walk 8 – **The Naze**

THE WALK

❶ Walk to the left of the snack kiosk and to the right of the Naze Tower. Go left at the Fire Beacon towards houses, then turn right taking the path by the shark, going slightly left. Cross a concrete drive and, keeping forward, eventually pass a spiral shell and go left to reach a pillbox.

❷ Continue right. At the next fork, turn right and then go left at the swordfish, keeping forward, ignoring side tracks, to reach another pillbox. Turn left here on a packed-clay path and keep forward downhill ignoring side paths. Reach the cliff edge and continue along it with the cranes of Harwich in the distance until you reach the sea wall.

❸ Go right, then left to climb up to the wall with a partial fence at the top. Now turn left on a surfaced path with a lagoon to your right. This is the start of the 2¾-mile sea wall section of the walk. After a while, the surfaced path disappears and a low iron wall lines the route. *At this point there is an opportunity for a short diversion; a path on the right enables you to visit the water edge when the tide is low, and it also gives an opportunity to observe sanderlings as they rush about churning up the mud for food.* Continue along beside Cormorant Creek and its associated lagoons and mudflats to reach an information board at Backwaters – this not only explains the association of the area with Arthur Ransome's *Secret Water*, but also suggests that there is a strong possibility of seeing seals here.

❹ Now you leave the North Sea to travel southwards alongside Walton Channel. To your left you can see the Naze Tower. As you progress, the Titchmarsh Marina, diagonally right with its host of masts, becomes more visible. Eventually you pass a redundant cycle barrier and a holiday rental on the right, The Lady of the Twizzle, to reach the end of the sea wall. Walk up the slope but, before the top, go left along another sea defence to reach a road (Hall Lane).

❺ For a shorter route (missing the pub) turn left up the hill along Naze Park Road and follow the route from point 6. For the full route, turn right along Hall Lane. When you reach the seafront keep ahead for the Bath House pub or turn sharp left along East Terrace to continue the walk. Follow the path behind the beach huts to join Cliff Parade, keeping straight ahead past a children's play area to reach Naze Park Road. If you prefer, walk along the length of the beach and rejoin the walk at the corner of Naze Park Road

20 Circular Walks in Essex

(dogs are not allowed on the beach between 1 May and 30 Sept).

6 Pass a children's playground and go right at the post box, then left along a narrow path overlooking the sea and chalets. Avoid the steps and fork left and go right at a T- junction; this wide track alongside big houses returns you to the car park.

Paul Farmer

9 Great Notley Country Park
3¾ miles (6 km)

Start: Great Notley Country Park, Great Notley. **Sat Nav:** CM77 7FS.
Parking: The pay and display car park at Great Notley Country Park. Follow the brown signs from the A131 and A120 for the main entrance.
Map: OS Explorer 195 Braintree & Saffron Walden. **Grid Ref:** TL736214.
Terrain: Mainly field-edge paths, manageable with all-terrain pushchairs, on the main walk. Once in the Park, the tracks are surfaced.

WALK HIGHLIGHTS

This relatively new Essex Country Park, with its trails, wildflower meadows, fishing lakes and more, all spread across 100 acres, offers a great day out. This walk whisks you away from the park at first for a pleasant amble through the countryside. I have little doubt that once you have visited you will return again and again.

20 Circular Walks in Essex

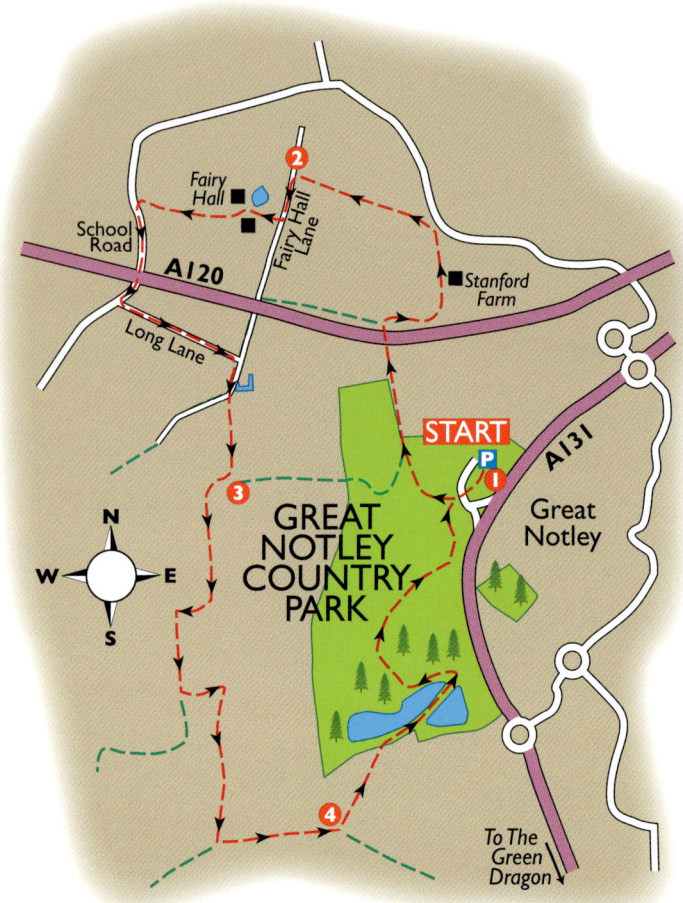

Walk 9 – **Great Notley Country Park**

REFRESHMENTS
The Green Dragon is a beamed, 18th-century pub serving a traditional menu under the Greene King umbrella. **Postcode:** CM77 8QN.
🌐 www.greeneking.co.uk/pubs/essex/green-dragon ☎ 01245 361030

THE WALK

❶ Return to the car park entrance. Go right and pass below the mound which houses the Discovery Centre and café (the parking pay stations are here). Keep going to the end of Sky Ropes and turn right on a waymarked, tree-lined path which will take you over the A120. Once over, immediately turn right down steps heading to a wooden bridge. Cross and turn left on a wide grassy track to go right of a gate and keep forward on a lane, passing Stanford Farm. Just before a road, turn left at a fingerpost. Keep forward across a field to join a fenced path which takes you to a lane (Fairy Hall Lane).

❷ Turn left, and then right through the gates of Fairy Hall. Before a metal gate, go left and then right alongside a barn. Turn left along a field-edge for 15m, then right at a post to a fenced path across the field onto a drive and the main road (School Road). Cross and go left to re-cross the A120 and turn left down Long Lane. Pass Toppersfield and go right at Spinners. When the track swings right, keep forward on a narrower path over grass then across a field to the next field.

❸ Go right along the hedge and then turn left, keeping the hedge on the right. Turn right and then left in the next field. At the boundary, go left and then right over a bridge with a large solar farm to the right. At the next boundary, turn left just before the bridge. Follow the field-edge and go through a gate onto a surfaced path.

❹ At the first junction turn left. Here you can see objects associated with the Discovery Trail. At the next junction go forward and then turn right with a lake on the left. Keep ahead to follow the lake edge as it curves left. Reach a black and white sign and go right on a surfaced path. Cross a bridge and keep with the path as it twists and turns. Cross another bridge and swing left, passing a fairy amongst trees. Reach a T-junction to go left and then right up to the Discovery Centre. Go down the steps and take the 3rd left to return to the car park.

10 Matching Tye
4¼ miles (6.7 km)

Start: The Fox Inn, The Green, Matching Tye. **Sat Nav:** CM17 0QS.
Parking: You may use the pub car park if you intend to visit. Alternatively, park around the triangular green.
Map: OS Explorer 183 Chelmsford & The Rodings. **Grid Ref:** TL515112.
Terrain: A short initial section along a road but mostly along and across fields; some uneven surfaces and three stiles.

WALK HIGHLIGHTS

'Matching' derives from Moecca Ing, Saxon for the 'meadow of the Moecca', with the Moecca being the tribe that ruled locally. The walk starts at Matching Tye, with its miniature green and splendid houses. Matching Green, as its name suggests, has a rather larger green with a cricket ground and pavilion, and is surrounded by beautiful buildings. The real treat here is Matching, whose picturesque trio of church, Marriage Feasting Hall and oak tree combine for one of the most recognisable images in Essex.

Walk 10 – **Matching Tye**

REFRESHMENTS
The Fox Inn is a good-value pub serving a range of beers and home cooked food.
🌐 www.thefoxinn.com ☎ 01279 731335

THE WALK

❶ Take the road signed to Matching Green, passing Gainsborough Cottage and Matthew's Chapel. After 170m, where the road swings sharply left, go right at a fingerpost and then right on a footpath which goes left at the wood. Just before the end of the field, go right and immediately left, heading away from the wood. Go left along the edge of an adjoining field to go through a gate to a road (Matching Tye Road).

❷ Turn right and, in 10m, turn right again along a left field-edge. Follow this as it goes left and right. Turn left at the end of a small wood and head across a bridge into the next field. Go straight to the nearest corner of the wood ahead. Where the trees end, keep forward, slightly left, to what appears to be the corner of woodland. As you get nearer you will see the waymarker which takes you along the left field-edge. Continue over a bridge, ignore a right fork and emerge at a stile and road (Matching Road).

❸ Cross over and turn left. When this main road swings left, go right. Join an obvious path on Matching Green which runs parallel with the road. Just before the Chequers you'll pass a blue-plaqued house which belonged to the artist Augustus John. Turn left opposite the pub and cross the cricket green, heading for the white signpost opposite. Turn left and left again after the pond, passing the village sign, and across the green to another signpost. At the junction, go forward to turn right, just before Wingates, along a hedged path. Head across the field to reach a surfaced cross-track.

❹ Turn left. At the boundary of Brick House Farm, turn right along a field edge, swing left then go right at another waymarker. Turn left to keep right of woodland. Now cross the field aiming for a yellow-topped waymarker about 70m to the right of a large barn. Cross a stile and walk up the left field-edge, alongside the 13th-century moat and Matching Hall, to a gate and lane (Church Road).

❺ Turn right with a cemetery on the left. Pass some wonderful old oak trees and a pond. When the lane swings right, go forward over a stile passing a

20 Circular Walks in Essex

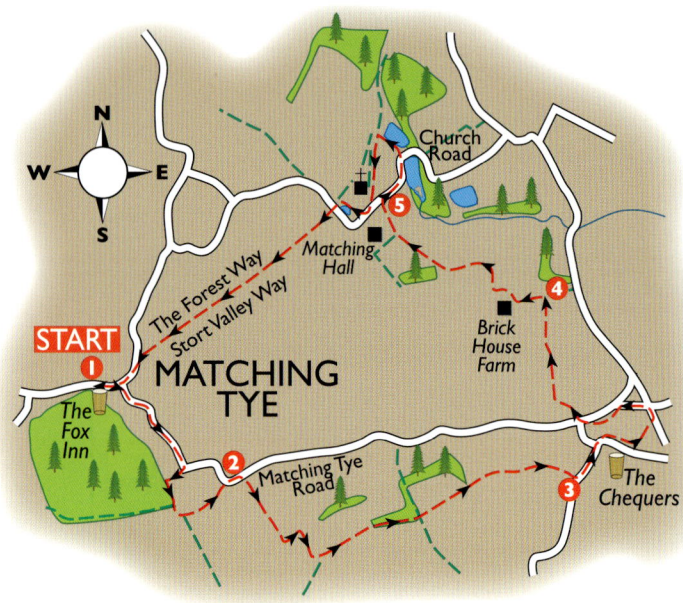

second pond towards the end of which you turn left and continue uphill to the boundary of the cemetery. Turn right here to reach a gate into the churchyard. Before a lane, turn right in front of the 13th-century Church of St Mary the Virgin and exit in front of the tree commemorating Queen Victoria's Jubilee. To the right is the 15th-century Marriage Feasting Hall (there are toilets at the end here). Walk forward to a concrete farm drive and turn right, passing a pond on the left after which you turn left at a fingerpost which indicates two promoted walks; the Forest Way and the Stort Valley Way. Keep ahead along the left field-edge to reach a road in just over ½ mile. Turn left to return to the pub and green.

11 Great Waltham
4 or 4½ miles (6.5 or 7.1 km)

Start: Hatchfields, Great Waltham. **Sat Nav:** CM3 1AJ.
Parking: Roadside parking in Hatchfields, a turning off Chelmsford Road on the eastern side of the village.
Map: OS Explorer 183 Chelmsford & The Rodings. **Grid Ref:** TL698134.
Terrain: Mainly well-drained field-edges on the outward journey, surfaced tracks on return. One stile. Dogs must be on a lead in the park.

WALK HIGHLIGHTS
Near the start and finish of this walk you'll encounter some of the most attractive scenes in Essex; a beautiful 16th-century timbered house, farm buildings, the River Chelmer and a country estate. Langleys, set in parkland and still privately owned, was built in 1719 and landscaped in 1814. Most of the route is back in the less-manicured countryside with a chance to visit the hamlet of Chatham Green and its curious windmill pub.

REFRESHMENTS
The Windmill is an upmarket pub and restaurant with a menu that is modern and seasonal. Take the longer route to pass the pub.
🌐 www.thewindmillchathamgreen.co.uk ☎ 01245 379545

20 Circular Walks in Essex

THE WALK

1 Walk back to Chelmsford Road, cross and turn right. In 100m turn sharp left at the Gate House to join a surfaced drive. You are now on the Langleys Estate amid parkland with impressive trees. Turn left at a fork with the main house to your right. Turn right through a metal kissing gate and continue to a second one ahead.

2 Turn right at the drive. Notice a submerged pillbox on the left and the way that the lower boughs of trees have been trimmed by grazing cattle. Pass a cemetery for house dogs, the striking stables and an icehouse on the right, and Coachman's Cottage on the left. Walk here in February and you will be astonished at the display of snowdrops on the banks of the River Chelmer which you cross. After a second bridge, immediately leave the drive and turn left along a Victorian metal fence. Go through a kissing gate and continue on a grassy path between fields and along a series of fine oaks. In ¼ mile reach a stile by a lane (Chatham Hall Lane).

3 Cross over and head diagonally right to continue along a left field-edge. Reach a main road (Essex Regiment Way). Cross with care to join the left field-edge opposite and keep forward to cross a bridge into a third field. Keep to the right of a group of trees to reach a path junction.

4 If visiting the Windmill pub, keep forward along a pleasant tree-lined path which takes you into the settlement of Chatham Green. Continue to a lane and turn right. Once refreshed, turn left out of the pub and then left again by the telegraph pole, passing the dovecote and following the hedged path back to the junction where you turn left. If you are continuing the walk without visiting the pub you will be turning right at this field junction. Go right across a bridge and forward along the side of another field and swing left with it to reach a gate and a lane (Scurvy Hall Lane). Turn right and keep forward through a partial barricade to reach the main road (Essex Regiment Way) in just under ½ mile.

5 Cross with care and re-join the lane. At a junction turn left then immediately right at a fingerpost passing another gatehouse to re-enter the Langleys estate. As the path swings left and crosses the bridge you re-join your outward path. Do not turn left just past the pet cemetery but continue along the drive. Just before reaching the gatehouse, turn left through the kissing gate. Cross the drive via two more kissing gates and continue to

Walk 11 – **Great Waltham**

another down in the corner of the pasture. At the road, turn left, past the Beehive pub on the right and the 12th-century church on the left. Swing left with the road with The Stores Café on the right. Don't miss Badynghams, a beautiful 16th-century house behind the war memorial. Take the first turning right to return to your car.

12 Langford & the Beeleigh Falls

4 miles (6.3 km)

Start: The Museum of Power, Hatfield Road, Langford. **Sat Nav:** CM9 6QA.
Parking: There is a free car park at the museum. Access via John Thresh Way.
Map: OS Explorer 183 Chelmsford & The Rodings. **Grid Ref:** TL835090.
Terrain: Mainly flat paths and tracks, some tree roots. Rain and/or high tides can make the going slippery and muddy. The drama of the falls is improved after heavy rain.

WALK HIGHLIGHTS

A pretty walk along the trackbed of a disused railway takes you from the village of Langford to the outskirts of Maldon. Here you cross the River Chelmer for the first time to start the return route, which is packed with interest. You'll pass the wonderful farmhouse of Beeleigh Abbey (built in 1570) and later the dramatic Beeleigh Falls near the confluence of the

Walk 12 – **Langford & the Beeleigh Falls**

Blackwater, Chelmer and Langford Cut. On your return, consider including a visit to the Museum of Power, with its magnificent Lilleshall Steam Pump, miniature railway and model village.

REFRESHMENTS
The Steam Pump Tea Room in the grounds of the museum provides breakfast and light lunches. ⊕ www.thesteampumptearoom.com. Alternatively, the Maldon Smokehouse has tables inside and out overlooking the river, along with a great menu. ⊕ www.maldonsmokehouse.co.uk ☎ 01621 212451

THE WALK

❶ From the museum car park, head along the concrete road, back towards the main road (Maldon Road/B1019) and turn right along the pavement. You will pass Langford Mill and a church. Where the pavement ends, feed in right onto the Blackwater Rail Trail. Pass the preserved Langford & Utley station platform and Elms Farm Park. Eventually the path swings right then left past an information board to a short drive.

❷ Cross, swinging slightly right to reach a short section of the Langford Cut. Ignore the footbridge and continue under the A414 to take the turning left into Oak Tree Meadow. Follow a surfaced path to the right and fork right at the children's play area. Turn right at the next junction to cross the Cut by a footbridge. Go left at the T-junction with Tesco on the left. At the end of the path, turn right and follow the road round to the right to meet the main road.

❸ Turn right and cross the River Chelmer and then immediately turn right again at the fingerpost by the buoy. Climb steps and turn right on a drive (Cromwell Lane), passing the Maldon Smokehouse on your right. Keep ahead on a grassy track, ignoring side paths. At the crosstracks, go right to go under the A414. Keep right at the junction along a tree-lined path which ends at a drive. On the immediate right is the privately-owned Beeleigh Abbey, occasionally open to the public.

❹ Reach a lane (Abbey Turning) and turn right. Continue past the 'no entry' sign and Beeleigh Falls House and on through a metal kissing gate with the remains of the water and steam mills on the right. Cross the Beeleigh Falls by a bridge and immediately fork right. At Beeleigh Lock turn right to cross the walkway. *Here you are crossing the confluence of two rivers: the Blackwater to the right of the fork and the Chelmer on the left.*

20 Circular Walks in Essex

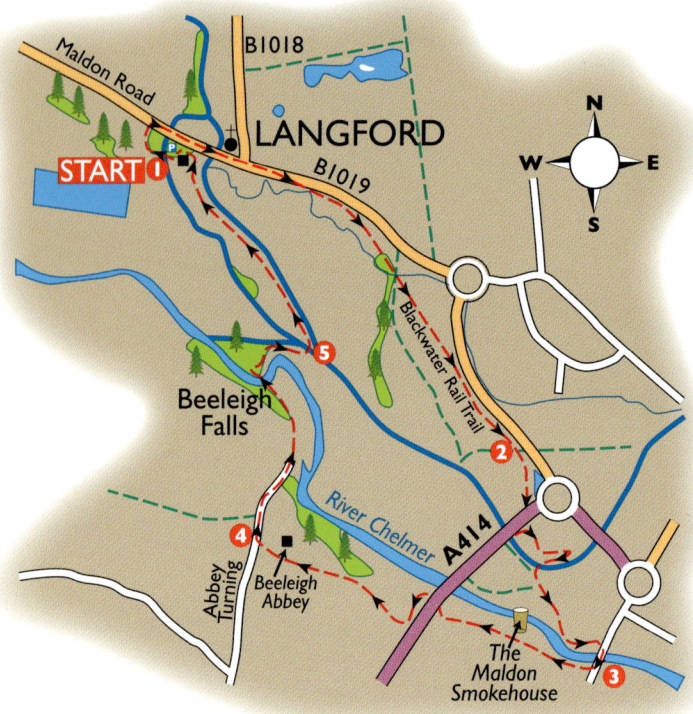

5 Turn left to cross the brick bridge. At the far end of a small parking area, go right along a waymarked path which follows the bank of the Langford Cut (visible in late autumn when the leaves have fallen). In just over ¼ mile join a surfaced drive and keep forward to reach a gate into the museum. Walk between buildings, turning left at the Station. Keep forward to return to your car passing the café and toilets.

13 Tollesbury Wick

5½ miles (9 km)

Start: : Free Car Park, Woodrolfe Road, Tollesbury. **Sat Nav:** CM9 8RY.
Parking: A free car park and toilets off Woodrolfe Road on the eastern side of the village.
Map: OS Explorer 176 Blackwater Estuary. **Grid Ref:** TL963106.
Terrain: Level footpaths which can be bumpy. Dogs on leads around the reserve. 2 stiles.

WALK HIGHLIGHTS

This is one of the easiest walks in the book to navigate as the bulk of it follows the coastal path around a sea wall. The boundary of the Wick is a salt marsh; a rich and diverse nature reserve that's home to many species of bird including marsh harriers, plover, lapwing, wigeon and oyster catcher. The best time to visit is in February although you must wrap up warmly as the winds on this exposed promontory are unforgiving. Besides the wildlife,

20 Circular Walks in Essex

the route checks off military paraphernalia, views out to the North Sea and boats galore.

REFRESHMENTS
The Harbour View, with its excellent views overlooking the marina, serves fresh home-cooked food and specialises in seafood.
🌐 www.the-harbour-view.co.uk ☎ 01621 869561

THE WALK

❶ Return to Woodrolfe Road and turn left, passing a series of cafés. Just before sail lofts you join an elevated footpath on the right. Soon you pass a free amenity pool where you can swim, build sandcastles, and have a picnic. Cross a concrete track with the Harbour View to your right. Continue on a fenced footpath, now with a tightly packed marina on the left. Pass a slipway and continue with a fence to your left. Reach a signposted junction. We will return on the right-hand path.

❷ Go left on the unfenced sea wall which you will follow in total for about 3 miles. On the left you can see the much-photographed red lightship which was retired in 1988. To the right there is a Second World War pillbox, the first of several you will see on the walk. Eventually the path swings right. On your left you look across the South Channel to see West Mersea in the distance. Reach a pillbox. *Ahead is the mouth of the River Blackwater entering the North Sea and on the other side is Bradwell Power Station against a wind farm background.*

❸ Continue with the Blackwater. Reach a gate and swing left over an inlet. The path goes right at another pillbox, directly ahead is Bradwell Marina. *Just past a more distant pillbox on the left, you will come to an information board – this describes a project, abandoned in 1921, which brought a railway to a pier; the metal gate to the right marks the end of the defunct route.*

❹ Leave the bank of the river and continue with Mill Creek to the left. Go through another gate and pass by an almost regal bench, Curly's Perch. Another 15m brings you to a path junction. Go right on a hedged path to leave the sea wall. Cross the stile and turn left on a farm track. There is an observation tower to the right. Keep forward across a junction at Wick Farm. A stile and gate take you onto a lane (Mell Road).

Walk 13 – **Tollesbury Wick**

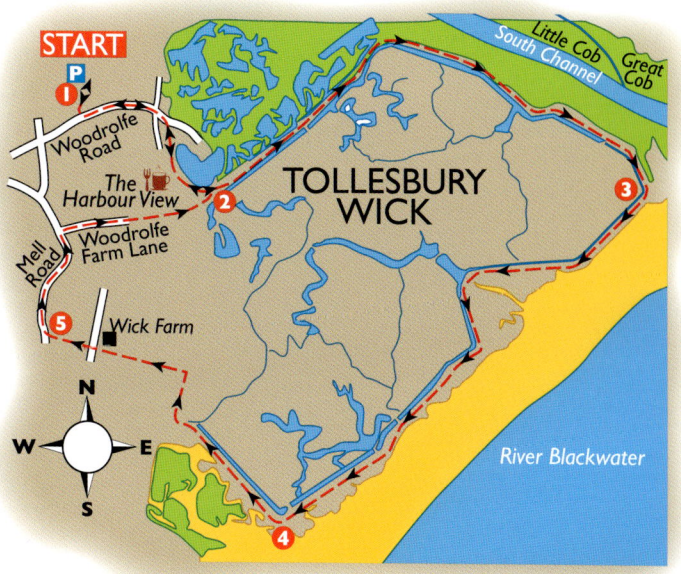

5 Turn right. Keep forward and just after a telephone kiosk, turn right on Woodrolfe Farm Lane. This becomes a stony drive and then a footpath which takes you to a junction passed earlier in the walk. Go left and keep to the edge of the marina, passing the Harbour View again, crossing the concrete drive to join the road and return to your car.

14 Waltham Abbey

5 ½ miles (9 km)

Start: Waltham Abbey Gardens car park, Abbey View, Waltham Abbey. **Sat Nav:** EN9 1XQ.
Parking: A pay and display car park off the main B194 roundabout.
Map: OS Explorer 174 Epping Forest & Lee Valley. **Grid Ref:** TL383008.
Terrain: Mainly tow paths and surfaced tracks. One section along a road.

WALK HIGHLIGHTS

This is a walk with much history, starting in the grounds of the last monastic house to be dissolved in 1540 under the Dissolution of the Monasteries Act. With some remains of the Augustinian Abbey still visible, you stroll through Waltham Abbey Gardens, passing the resting place of King Harold II along the way, before heading for the River Lee Navigation with its superb canal-side views.

REFRESHMENTS

The Crown, which you'll pass towards the end of the walk, serves home-cooked food and particularly good roasts.
🌐 www.thecrownpubwa.co.uk ☎ 01992 732590

Walk 14 – **Waltham Abbey**

THE WALK

1 Facing the abbey wall, go right along the paved avenue of trees. Emerge and then turn left across grass to a ruined gateway. Once through leave the path and go diagonally right towards the abbey where you will reach the grave of King Harold II. Go to the left of the abbey and join the path to continue along the main road. Cross to the left-hand side before the roundabout but keep forward. Return to the right-hand side at the pedestrian crossing and pass the entrance to the Gunpowder Mills. Cross a bridge over the Horsemill Stream and turn right immediately. Go left across grass, passing the skeleton of a Viking ship and cross the Lee Valley Navigation via the lock bridge.

2 Turn right on the towpath. Go under a bridge and in just over ½ mile you will reach Waltham Common Lock No10. Cross over the bridge, go right and swing left, crossing two bridges to continue alongside the Powdermill Cut. Soon after a pillbox, ignore one junction and continue to a T-junction.

3 Turn left onto Walton's Walk, named after Izaak Walton who referred to this stretch in his book *The Compleat Angler*. Keep the Horsemill Stream, a flood-relief channel, to your right and in ½ mile you will reach a car park.

4 Turn sharp left, cross a bridge and continue between lakes to reach a Viking fingerpost, which refers to a legend that King Alfred the Great left a Viking raiding party stranded here when he diverted the course of the River Lee. Keep forward to cross the Lee Navigation, then turn right to join the towpath and go right under the bridge you have just crossed. Pass the climbing wall, the boat racks and the lakes of the Young Mariners' Centre. At Waltham Common Lock No 10 go right over a bridge then immediately left passing a wood sculpture of the Green Man. Cross a bridge with Bowyer's Water to your right. If you are lucky, following narrow paths to the left, you may see some Old English goats – these have been imported from the Cheviot to keep the scrub down. Keep left at a fork and at the T-junction go left. Cross a bridge and keep to the surfaced path continuing right alongside the railings of the White Water Centre to eventually enter by a gate on the right which takes you to the canoe pool. Turn right and head for Reception by swinging left and right.

5 Enter and go up the stairs on the left (there are toilets on the left at the top). Go through doors onto The Terrace. Keep forward to join a path which is bounding the water course. If the Centre is in operation, you will get excellent

20 Circular Walks in Essex

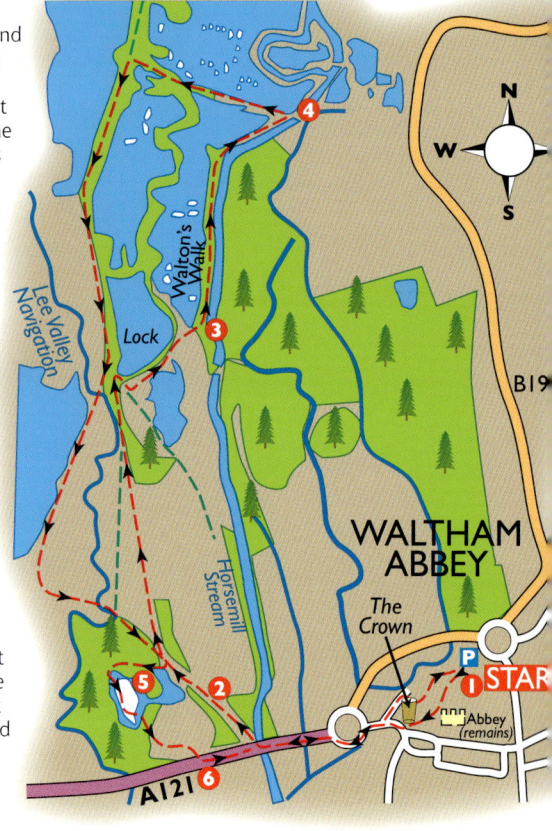

views of rafts and kayaks battling against the hazards of what was used for the 2012 Olympics competitions. Keep to this, ignoring a bridge and going right at The Finish Line Café. You will join a wider road through car parking and go right to the main road (Station Road).

❻ Turn left and head for the abbey which you can see in the distance. About 70m before the abbey, turn left along Romeland passing the Crown pub, keeping to the right to cross one bridge, then another. In the field, go left through a gap and right on a surfaced path passing ruins of the abbey. Just past a small café, go right at a paved junction to enter a garden. Fork left, then go right to return to the car park.

15 Epping Forest
3 miles (5 km)

Start: : Royal Forest Hotel, Ranger's Road, Epping Forest. **Sat Nav:** E4 7QH.
Parking: If you are intending to visit the Royal Forest Hotel before or after your walk, you can leave your car in its car park; otherwise, use the pay and display Barn Hoppitt Car Park opposite.
Map: OS Explorer 174 Epping Forest & Lee Valley. **Grid Ref:** TQ396947.
Terrain: There are several indistinct paths on the outward journey which will be navigable with all-terrain pushchairs. Watch out for tree roots, uneven surfaces and mud after rain. Good for dogs and no stiles. [There are toilets at the Visitor Centre].

WALK HIGHLIGHTS
No book about walks in Essex would be complete without at least one route through Epping Forest. This one comes with some added interest. In the days of Henry VIII, hunting was also something of a spectator sport. Thus the Queen Elizabeth Hunting Lodge, which is near the start of the walk, served as a kind of VIP lounge for royal guests and hangers-on to watch as the chase passed below in the valley. When the lodge was first built, the upper storey was open to the elements.

20 Circular Walks in Essex

REFRESHMENTS
The Royal Forest Hotel has an extensive menu, including plenty of popular children's options.
🌐 www.brewersfayre.co.uk/en-gb/locations/greater-london/royal-forest
☎ 0208 5237246

THE WALK
❶ With your back to the main hotel entrance, go left along the pavement past the wooden-clad Butler's Retreat. Turn left to a drinking fountain. Go right and fork right passing a pond on the right. Fork right again and keep right on a fairly indistinct path. Eventually reach a group of trees then a cross-path. Turn right and keep forward to a ride with a barrier next to the road. NB, 'rides' are surfaced tracks for horses.

❷ Go left on the ride. When you reach a cross-track turn right towards the edge of Connaught Water, constructed in 1893 to drain a swamp. Turn right to follow the edge of the lake round, past a car park, and onto a wooden walkway which you follow.

❸ Keep forward across a path and between a group of three large trees then swing right on a path. Keep forward on this clear, meandering path to reach a ride.

❹ Cross diagonally right. Keep forward at a cross-track into a group of trees. Later the path swings right through grassland. Take the first side path on the right, passing through trees and emerging on a redundant road (Fairmead Road).

❺ Turn left and then left again along a ride which swings left. Ignore a right fork. At the next junction, swing left with the main ride, then right to pause opposite a large tree on the right. This is the Grimston's Oak, one of only two trees in the whole of Epping Forest to have a name. Find a path left. Keep right at a fork to reach the edge of Connaught Water.

❻ Turn right. Continue to the point

Walk 15 – **Epping Forest**

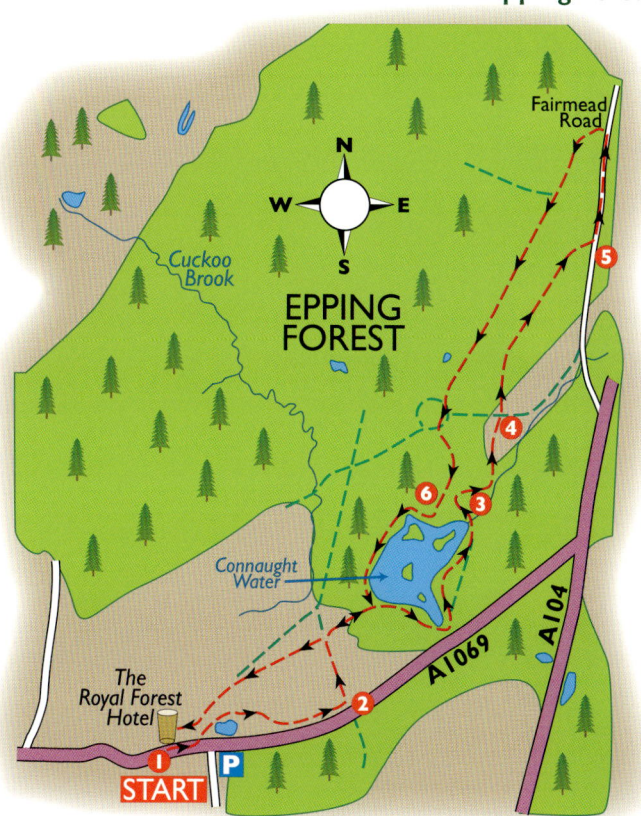

where you joined the water's edge earlier; turn right down the slope to reach a cross-track. Keep forward over grass, heading to the right of a large bushy area. Stay on the path as it swings to the left uphill with Butler's Retreat to your left and exit through a gate by ornamental deer to pass the Queen Elizabeth Hunting Lodge. Go right past the visitor centre to return to the Royal Forest Hotel.

16 Weald Country Park

2½ miles (4.2 km)

Start: Weald Country Park Visitor Centre Car Park, Weald Road. **Sat Nav:** CM14 5QX.
Parking: There are four car parks in the vicinity of the park, the one we are starting from is pay and display called the 'Visitor Centre Car Park'. There are toilets and an electric car charging point.
Map: OS Explorer 175 Southend & Basildon. **Grid Ref:** TQ569941.
Terrain: The paths are mostly good and can be managed by pushchairs. Dogs should be kept on a lead so as not to trouble the wildfowl and, especially, the fallow deer (these are wandering all over the park as evidenced by their tracks and droppings). There are plenty of seats and picnic places.

WALK HIGHLIGHTS

This walk is an introduction to another of the superb Essex country parks. Here you will pass a beautiful lake populated with a wide range of waterfowl, climb gently to woodland that houses many ancient oaks, and descend over grassland with a distinct possibility of seeing deer. Young people are well catered for with four play areas and a visit to the deer park can't fail to entertain.

Walk 16 – **Weald Country Park**

REFRESHMENTS
The Wigley Bush Café, adjoining the Visitor Centre, serves hot and cold snacks. For a more substantial meal you might try the Nag's Head on Brook Street which is 1½ miles away. (**Postcode:** CM14 5ND).
🌐 www.thenagsheadbrentwood.co.uk ☎ 01277 260005

THE WALK

❶ Head to the back of the car park and turn left downhill on a surfaced track. Keep forward with a lake on your right and the deer park on your left. At the end, cross a footbridge and continue with the lake on your right. Reach the end of the lake with a playground on the left.

❷ Go left at the junction, taking the second track which is just inside the Forest. Keep forward, climbing gradually uphill, between magnificent trees. At the top, turn right along a path labelled 'pedestrians only'. Ignore the right turn by an information board, but fork left later to pass some fir trees. Cross a stream and arrive at a T-junction.

❸ Go right and turn left in front of a fence with a treehouse beyond. Cross a second stream and turn right. Go over a bridge and uphill, swinging gradually right. At the top of the rise, go straight ahead on a narrow path. Head through a gate and keep forward across grassland (keep a lookout for deer here; there are also often cattle grazing). Keep with the grassy path through woodland. Emerge to go diagonally right, then right in front of a six-bar gate, and cross a bridge, through a gate and turn left.

20 Circular Walks in Essex

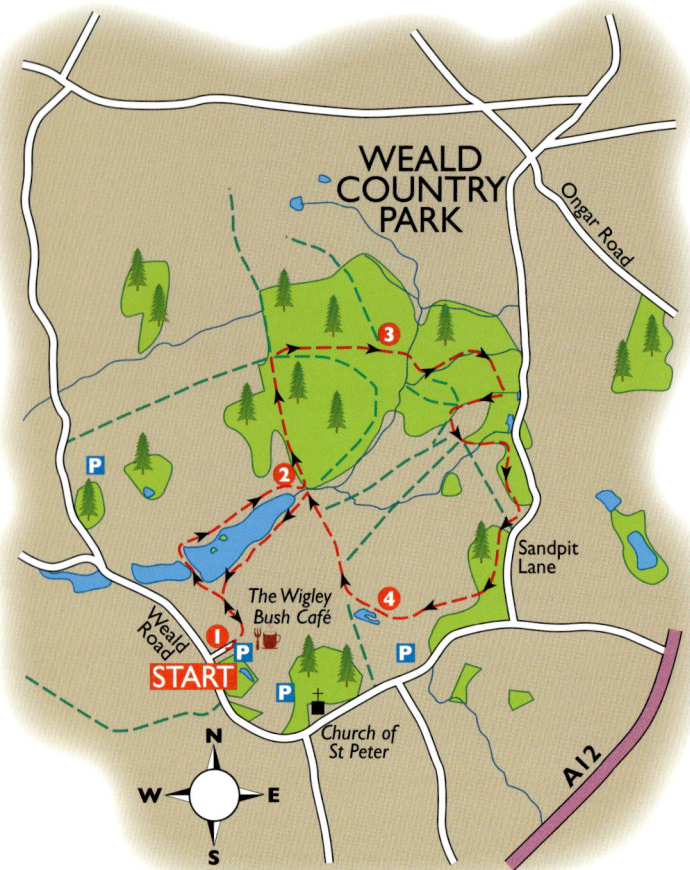

❹ Fork left and follow the path alongside the lake which is on your right. At the end, turn left and walk up the hill with the Church of St Peter on the horizon. Return to the car park.

17 RSPB Rainham Marshes
1½ or 2 miles (2.2 or 3.5 km)

Start: RSPB Rainham Marshes, New Tank Hill Road, Purfleet. **Sat Nav:** RM19 1SZ.
Parking: There is a large free car park at RSPB Rainham Marshes, but donations are encouraged.
Map: OS Explorer 162 Greenwich & Gravesend. **Grid Ref:** TQ548788.
Terrain: The route is almost equally divided between semi-surfaced paths and boardwalks both of which can be travelled by pushchairs. There is always the possibility of diversions, and these will be well signed. This is open country so wrap up warmly during the winter months. Dog-friendly.

WALK HIGHLIGHTS
This portion of Rainham Marshes, Aveley Marsh, was purchased by the RSPB in 2006 and its subsequent development into a nature reserve was inspirational: accessible routes were built with a wealth of information boards along the way; beautiful and idiosyncratic hides were provided, along with viewpoint mountings; and young people were catered for with a play area and interpretation boards. This is probably the best site for birdwatching in Essex, so remember to take your binoculars.

Note: it is only possible to do this walk during the opening hours of the reserve. Check the website for details.

20 Circular Walks in Essex

REFRESHMENTS
There is a pleasant café at the Visitor Centre or you could take a picnic to have at one of the many designated areas during the walk. The nearest pub is the Royal Hotel, ¼ mile walk along the river, which boasts a lovely riverside location.
🌐 www.theroyalpurfleet.co.uk ☎ 01708 860852

THE WALK
❶ Walk to the far end of the car park and use the stairs or lift of the visitor centre (there are toilets on the right at the bottom) turn right and enter the café, go right to exit at the door by the shop at the end. Descend by a surfaced track to go left at the junction. Soon join a boardwalk on the right which takes you to the Purfleet Hide where you can view birds on what is known as the Purfleet Scrape. Continue on a surfaced path to reach the Discovery Zone via more boardwalk.

❷ The Zone also contains a hide with seating which enables you to relax with a panoramic view and panels explaining the history of the marsh development for children. Continue the walk via reed beds. Shortly after crossing a channel, you will reach a model anthill with a lapwing scrape on the top. There are also picnic facilities. As you proceed you will pass, on the left, a one-way turnstile. Here you can shorten your walk by going through the turnstile, taking a narrow path (inaccessible to pushchairs) and turning left back towards the visitor centre with views of the Thames Estuary and the Dartford Crossing. For the longer route, keep following the path as it swings to the right. Ahead you will see large-numbered shooting butts. Before the butts, there is sometimes a small clearing on the left where bearded tits feed on a table.

❸ *Opposite is a bank of metal which protected those raising the targets from these butts. Some winding gear used for the operation still exists and old, faded paintings illustrate those activities. Further along you will encounter a short, narrow path on the left which leads to the target pools. This was where soldiers practiced throwing hand grenades, now it is a superb viewing point to watch lapwings. On the right is Shooting Butts Hide which has windows in all directions and a collection of artefacts discovered on the marshes.* Continue past Shooting Butts Hide to join a boardwalk which takes you past a couple of viewpoints. Keep ahead on a semi-surfaced path and cross a track to reach Ken Barrett Hide.

Walk 17 – RSPB Rainham Marshes

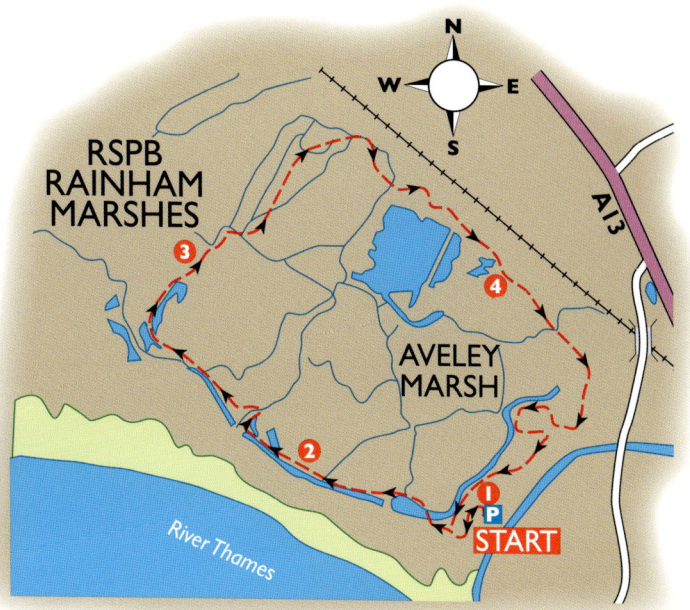

④ Keep forward over a track to join another boardwalk which takes you through a densely reeded area then turn right at the windmill to join a grassy path alongside a stream. Reach a junction and go right then turn left through a tunnel, these are the remains of one of several cordite stores. At the next junction, go right then left along a narrower path to the children's play area (you can by-pass the narrower path by keeping forward). Re-emerge at a junction with the main path. Keep forward to climb gradually up to the visitor centre, walk through the café, descend the steps on the left, and return to your car.

18 Hylands Estate
2 miles (3.1 km)

Start: Hylands Estate, London Road, Writtle, Chelmsford. **Sat Nav:** CM2 8WQ.

Parking: The entrance to the estate is brown signed off the A414 (Greenbury Way) near Widford. There are two pay and display car parks but the walk starts from the one on the left of the drive.

Map: OS Explorer 183 Chelmsford & The Rodings. **Grid Ref:** TL681048.

Terrain: The first half of the walk is on unmarked routes across grassland so directions should be read carefully. The return is on semi-surfaced paths. The whole walk is fairly flat and manageable by all-terrain pushchairs. Dogs should be on a lead near the lake and House.

WALK HIGHLIGHTS

Hylands is an attractive Grade II-listed public park under the ownership of Chelmsford City Council. The main house was built towards the end of the 18th century and is open to the public on selected days. However, this walk explores some of the ancient woodland, lake, formal Victorian gardens and spectacular grounds, much of which were landscaped by Humphry Repton.

Walk 18 – **Hylands Estate**

REFRESHMENTS
The Deli Hylands, located at the Stables near the main house, has a good menu offering breakfast and lunch. There are also often free band performances on weekends.
🌐 www.hylandsestate.co.uk/explore/thedelihylands ☎ 01245 357770

THE WALK
❶ From the car park, head to the fingerpost signed to Serpentine Lake. Aim for the left-hand corner of the furthest of two clumps of trees ahead. Just before arriving at the trees, turn right along their edge. At the end of the clump, go left along its lower edge, then continue in a straight line towards the slender spire of Widford church ahead. Keep to the left of the trees ahead to reach the lake on the right.

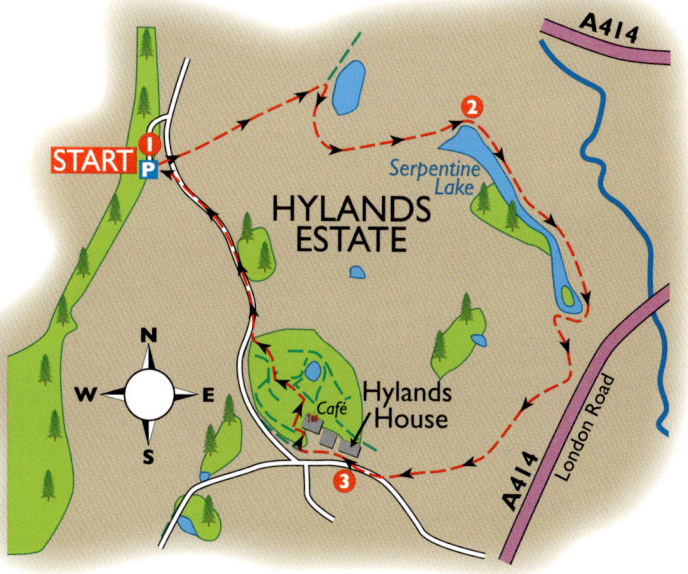

20 Circular Walks in Essex

❷ Turn right to walk along a well-worn path alongside Serpentine Lake. Turn right at the end of the lake towards an information board, a bench, and a surfaced path. Turn left and follow the path to a T-junction where you go right. Soon you will approach Hylands House. At the intersection of paths, turn right and, after crossing the ha-ha, pass the spectacular entrance.

❸ Fork right and then turn right to the Stables. *Here you'll find art studios, an information point, shops, toilets, and a café; this is a dog-free area but a little further on you will pass an extension of the café which welcomes pets.* Continuing from the Stables, go right at a fork and right again to enter the Pleasure Gardens. You can explore further but we will be exiting from the far-left corner. Turn left here to a T-junction where a right turn takes you back to the starting point of the walk and the car park. If you have children with you, beyond the toilets in the larger car park there is a magnificent play castle which is deemed safe for children of 2 to 12 years.

19 Two Tree Island

2¼ miles (3.4 km)

Start: Two Tree Island Car Park, High Street, Castle Point District. **Sat Nav:** SS9 2GB.
Parking: From Leigh-on-Sea Station turn south away from Belton Way and keep on this road, passing car parks, until you can go no further to reach a large, free car park on a wharf.
Map: OS Explorer 175 Southend-on-Sea & Basildon. **Grid Ref:** TQ823848.
Terrain: Uneven surfaces, possible with all-terrain buggies. Dog-friendly.

WALK HIGHLIGHTS

Named after two elm trees blown over in the 1960s, Two Tree Island is reached by a bridge that takes you onto a wilderness surrounded by mudflats. Criss-crossed by paths and surprisingly rich in vegetation, it now supports a nature reserve that has become an important resting place for migrating birds. The prize is to see the now-comparatively-rare avocets that nest in the area, but there are many more birds and animals to be observed.

The site, which covers 300 hectares, can absorb hundreds of visitors and still seem deserted. On a clear day you can see Hadleigh Castle, Canvey Island and the pier at Southend.

20 Circular Walks in Essex

REFRESHMENTS
The Golf Range Café, on the right just before the bridge onto the island, serves rolls and hot drinks. An alternative would be to make a slight detour for the Crooked Billet on the High Street in Leigh-on-Sea (SS9 2EP), where you'll find hearty pub fare and excellent seafood.
🌐 www.nicholsonspubs.co.uk/restaurants/eastofengland/thecrookedbilletleighonsea ☎ 01702 480289

THE WALK

❶ Before starting, it is worth heading down onto the slipway for views across to Canvey Island. Go back to the car park entrance and walk a short distance up the road to a fingerpost and turn right onto the coastal path. Take an early fork right through a wooden barrier (note information about adders). Keep forward down steps to walk alongside an inlet. On the left you are likely to see ducks, geese and moorhens and on the mudflats to your right, there is usually a mass of sea birds feeding on the eel grass. Reach the end of the inlet.

❷ After a few metres, turn left and follow a waymarker and then turn left at the next. Go through a barrier by a six-bar gate and turn right by a waymarker just before the lane. Reach a car park.

❸ Go diagonally left across the lane to a gate. Immediately take the right fork. Eventually you will join a semi-surfaced path and may well hear the

Walk 19 – Two Tree Island

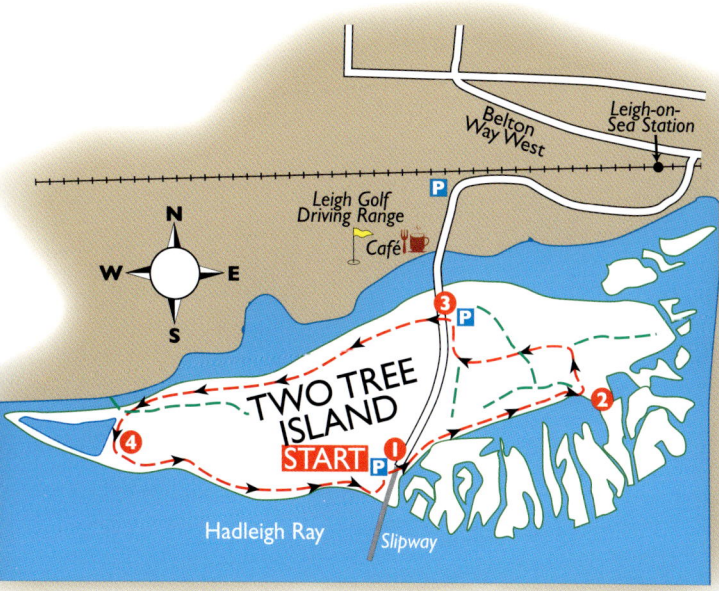

sound of model aircraft being flown on the left and have views of Hadleigh Castle and the Olympic mountain bike track to the right. At the next waymarker, go forward, ignoring the left turn. Continue to ignore left turns as you get closer to the channel on the right. Finally the path swings left by a waymarker. Another path leads down to a potential crossing of the channel which can be used at low tide. Soon you will reach a hide from which you can look out onto the salt lagoon. *You will always see a number of birds here but wintertime is when black-tailed godwit, curlew, redshank, and dunlin flock here. The star of the show is the avocet with its curious upturned beak.*

❹ Continue on from the hide. From here, you can see Southend Pier ahead and you may see large ships on the Thames Estuary. At a junction by a bench, fork right. Ignore the next waymarked path and any others off to the left and head back to the car park.

20 RSPB Wallasea Island
6 miles (9.6 km)

Start: Wallasea Island Car Park. **Sat Nav:** SS4 2HD. Follow the brown tourism signs to RSPB Wallasea Island.
Parking: At the free car park on RSPB Wallasea Island.
Map: OS Explorer 176 Blackwater Estuary. **Grid Ref:** TQ955945.
Terrain: Most of the walk is on sea walls making the route quite exposed, so wrap up warmly. Dogs are not allowed on most of the site.

WALK HIGHLIGHTS

The RSPB have created wildlife-rich salt marsh, lagoons and mudflats here, in an amazing project that has transformed the coastline. Three million tonnes of earth, dug up during excavations for the construction of London's Elizabeth line, were used in the process. You will see masses of birds all year round, but the best time to visit is a clear, sunny winter's day. With luck you may even see seals in the estuaries.

Walk 20 – **RSPB Wallasea Island**

REFRESHMENTS
The award-winning Shepherd & Dog is about 2½ miles back along the road to Rochford, at Ballards Gore. This is a popular pub where you can expect a warm welcome and locally sourced food. **Sat Nav:** SS4 2DA.
🌐 theshepherdanddogstambridge.co.uk ☎ 01702 258658

THE WALK
❶ Go to the far end of the car park, through the gate on the left-hand side and up the slope to the sea wall. Ahead is the River Crouch and directly opposite is bustling Burnham-on-Crouch. Turn right to walk along the grassy-topped sea wall with the salt marsh to your left and grasslands to the right. Diagonally left you will see a substantial wind farm and you will pass the RSPB headquarters below on the right. After about ¾ mile the sea wall swings to the right.

❷ To your left you can see where the original sea wall was breached. Keep ahead following the coastal path then fork right at the next junction. Soon you will be able to see the settlement of Churchend on Foulness Island

20 Circular Walks in Essex

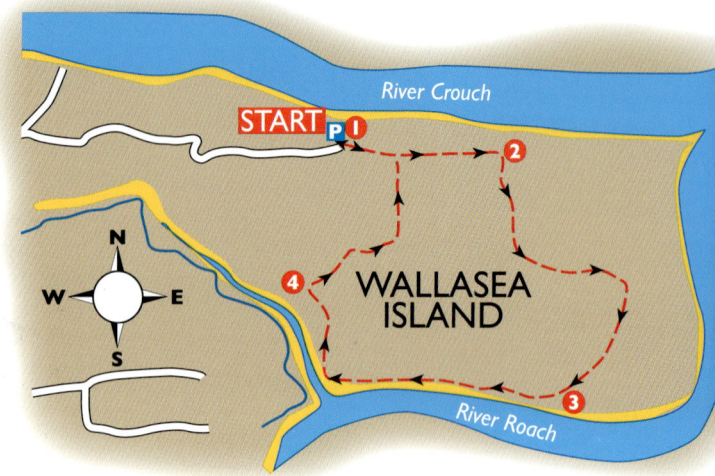

ahead of you and encounter an amusing signpost indicating a whole range of destinations. Eventually you arrive at Half Moon viewpoint which acts as a shelter and a hide.

❸ Turn right with the fingerpost signed to the car park, but this time keep below the sea wall. Opposite Old Pool, the path rises almost up to the sea wall; now you have the River Roach on your left with the outline of Rochford ahead. When the path swings right away from the Roach you can look across to Paglesham Eastend. An information board relates the history of HMS *Beagle* and its subsequent demise off Paglesham Pool – with a brief mention of Charles Darwin. Reach a fingerpost where the sea wall curves left.

❹ Turn right, signed to the car park. Fork left to take a grassy path, passing solar panels which power an irrigation system. Continue forward at a junction with a track coming in from the right. Here there is another information point with a flimsy hide which overlooks the Acresfleet lagoons. Keep following the signs to the car park and later waymarkers. At a T-junction, turn left to return to the car park.